A Glimpse of God's Heart

How Trying to Change My Kids Changed Me

Kevin & Julie,
Keep splashing grace

Claudia Fletcher

ISBN: 978-0-615-31538-6

Printed in the United States of America.

to my husband Bart,
who show's God's heart to me,
to our congregation,
and to our children every day.

Acknowledgements

Special thanks . . .

again to my husband. He's incredible. There is no way that I could do anything I do without Him. I could spend pages telling you how wonderful he is.

to my kids who put up with their mom being behind a computer screen way too often and who have taught me so much about God's heart.

to those who helped edit this book. Tom, Brenda, Peter, and Jodi. The fact that you were willing to read, critique, proofread, and return chapters back to me at record speed kept me motivated and encouraged throughout the process. And to those who read sections of the book, Dawn, Leah and Janet, along with various Facebook friends and gave me feedback. You are awesome!

to my parents who continue to be a daily inspiration;

to my friends.... past and present...in person and online...who support me even though I am still so "rough around the edges."

and to God who, through His Son Jesus, offers us grace beyond measure. It is such a comfort to me to know that there is nothing I can do to make Hm love me more and that there is nothing I could do that would make Him love me less.

Introduction

The fact that my husband and I have 12 children is a clear indication that I don't plan far enough ahead or think much about details. Adopting children from foster care and a third-world orphanage seemed like an excellent way to passionately live out my faith. The fact that I hate to clean house, I can't cook, I despise laundry and I really don't especially enjoy being around kids didn't seem to matter during those years when I was busy acquiring them. I was so fired up about changing the world that it slipped my mind!

Fortunately, I have a husband who loves to cook and grocery shop (and is such an excellent chef and baker that he is solely responsible for at least 500 of the pounds that I have gained repeatedly between diets over the past 15 years). He doesn't mind cleaning, does a better job with laundry than I do and is a wonderful father who truly delights in his children. With all those things going for us, we have managed to survive our first 14 years of parenting.

Another clue that I may not have been thinking ahead is the fact that we have had, at some points in time, nine teenagers at one time. When I was in graduate school and beginning my career, one supervisor often said, "Prior, proper planning prevents pitifully poor performance." I obviously was not paying attention.

A GLIMPSE OF GOD'S HEART

Five years into our adoption journey, we had claimed nine children ages 4-14. My mother, who was older when she gave birth to me and my two brothers, was sharing wisdom with me and decided it was time to let me know that teenagers and menopause do not mix. I pointed out to her that it was a bit late to share that news, as far more teenagers than anyone should have at any given time and "the change" were going to collide in very big way several years down the road. So when it finally hit me a few years ago that I should have been a bit more deliberate in my planning, it was a little too late.

During the past year or two I have found myself surrounded not only by teenagers, but by adult children making choices very different from those I had dreamed for them. In fact, they were heading down roads I had warned them about; roads that were far from anything I had recommended or advised. Nothing I had ever said seemed to matter. There was nothing I could do to make them be the people I had hoped they would be. The harder I tried to change them, the more resistant they were to change. Suddenly my entire life seemed like less of a good idea.

But as my husband and I struggled through months in the valley battling regret, frustration, disillusionment and discouragement, one thing became very clear. While I had set out on a journey to change the world by changing a few children, God's agenda was far different. All along it had been His plan to change me by giving me glimpses into His character as I attempted to deal lovingly with children who were about as malleable as I am.

Maybe you are currently walking through a valley that has been a result of your choices. Possibly you've been more careful, planning well for a life of ease, when uninvited trouble, pain and struggle have burst into your life unannounced and taken you by surprise. Regardless of the challenges you face, know that God is with you, waiting to give you a clearer understanding of His nature -- His unconditional love, His everlasting peace, His infinite wisdom, His abundant joy and His amazing grace.

Join me at my favorite coffee house and grab a latte or flavored blend of coffee, a smoothie, or a glass of iced tea. Let me share my story and explain to you, in simple terms, the things I have learned. It is my hope and prayer that while we visit, God will change your heart as you see a clearer picture of His heart.

I join the Apostle Paul in saying, *"In all my prayers for all of you, I always pray with joy because of your partnership in the gospel from the first day until now, being confident of this, that he who began a good work in you will carry it on to completion until the day of Christ Jesus."* Philippians 1:4-6

God's Unconditional Love

1

God's Adopting Love

For those of you who have experienced the miracle of adoption, you will not be surprised at how much being an adoptive parent has taught me about God. As Bart and I have claimed 12 children as our own, we have been reminded again and again of the fact that we are the adopted children of God.

On eight different occasions over a 12-year period, we met a child or group of children who were strangers to us. One was a toddling 20-month-old with big blue eyes and a tentative smile who explored his new world with apprehension. Another, with wisps of blonde hair peeking out of a snow cap, in a pink snowsuit even though he was clearly a boy, was placed on my lap at the age of 9 months. Bright orange hair proclaiming his Irish heritage, an 8-year-old and his 11-year-old brother had their daily activities interrupted by our arrival when we came to meet them for the first time.

Three charming Hispanic children ran across their foster home to jump in our arms at the ages of 8, 6 and 4 on a crisp winter day in New Mexico. A shy boy of 11 with curly hair sat alone at his residential treatment center, his cascading curls a tribute to his biracial identity, when we drove up for our introduction. A tour around his Guatemalan orphanage provided a gregarious 9-year-old the opportunity to get to know us, and it was on that trip we met for the first time a quiet, subdued 6-year-old who would become ours four years later. And a fall day in Texas just three years ago brought us into contact with two of the most beautiful boys we had ever seen, bright dark eyes in the midst of warm, tan complexions, as they, considered too old to adopt by many, entered our world at the ages of 8 and 12.

All of these children were strangers to us. They had not chosen to be our children, but a system of big people had made decisions without consulting them. They were suddenly part of our lives and were ready to see if we would love them regardless of their behaviors. Many of our older children had already been moved from one foster care placement to another because the parents in that home could not handle their special needs. They entered prepared to get things over with and set themselves up for another rejection.

But we had been trained that we needed to claim our children as ours from the day we met them. The idea of them ever having to leave our homes or to cease being our children was never an option for us. So as we struggled through years of behaviors, psychiatric hospitalizations, juvenile detention centers, drug treatment, false accusations and the daily drain of living with children with challenges, we remained fiercely committed to them.

Prior to adopting our children, I had studied the book of Romans in depth. In chapter 8, verse 15, Paul writes: "*For you did not receive a spirit that makes you a slave again to fear, but you received the Spirit of sonship. And by him we cry, "Abba, Father.*"" While the idea of God becoming my "Daddy" was a touching thought, it was the adoption of our children, each situation unique, that helped me grasp what it really meant to have God claim me as His own.

A court hearing to finalize the adoption of a child includes several questions. One of them is, "Do you understand that if you adopt this child you will have the same responsibilities as if this child was born to you?" In addition to this, the child automatically receives the same rights as if he had been born to these parents. In fact, legally, in many states, it is not legal to exclude an adopted child from an estate plan or will, while a birth child may be so excluded.

As I sat in court on eight separate occasions, I was able to finally understand what it meant to have God adopt me. As I realized that my children now belonged to me as if I had given birth to them, I understood for the first time, very clearly, that I belonged to God in a way that was no different than the way in which Jesus belongs to God.

Adoption means that God has claimed you and that you are no different than Jesus in God's eyes. You now have the same exact rights as God's son Jesus! It means that you don't have to be afraid to crawl up into his lap when you need a hug. It means that you can have an intimate relationship with him, where you call Him Daddy. It means that there is nothing you can't ask Him, nothing He wouldn't do for you. You are HIS.

And as His child, you are also His heir... an heir to everything that belongs to God. Your adoption by the King of Heaven and Earth means that all He has belongs to you. His earth is yours to enjoy. His riches are yours for the asking. His love for you goes beyond anything you could imagine. Abundant and amazing, this BIG God is your Daddy. He has adopted you and you are entitled to everything that is His.

It could be that your earthly father wasn't the kind of Dad you wished he could be and for years you have struggled with this concept of God as Father. For people in this case, adoption can be even more meaningful. All of our children have two earthly fathers. They have a birthfather who for one reason or another could not be part of their lives as children. They have their father, the man who claimed them through adoption to belong to him. He is the one who has bandaged scraped knees, been to school conferences, read to them, helped with homework, and acted as cheerleader at countless sporting events. He is their dad because of the gift of adoption.

God has already claimed you as His child. There is nothing you must do in order to earn this and you cannot stop Him from claiming you. It has been God's decision from the beginning.

When our son Tony was four years old we finalized his adoption and soon after planned for his baptism. As my husband talked with him in simple terms, he explained to him that when we are baptized we are asking Jesus to live in our hearts. Tony seemed to grasp the concept when it was initially explained to him. On the day of his baptism, Bart asked Tony again, "Do you remember what baptism means, Tony?" To which he responded, "Yeah, Dad. It means that I'm living in God's heart."

God's adoption of us means just that. It means that you and I live in His heart. He has claimed you and you are His. He has adopted you as His child. You belong to Him. Relax and let that thought sink in as you climb into his lap, settle in, and realize that you are indeed a child of the King.

2

God's Patient Love

In the adoption community we have good reason to talk frequently about attachment and bonding. We are parents of children who have spent their first years of life without forming a proper attachment to their primary caregivers, and thus they struggle with relationships throughout their lives. This unfortunate situation is not something the children choose any more than they can "un-choose" it as they grow older, but it impacts them and us deeply.

Most parents are able to handle the attachment piece with newborns fairly naturally. If their lives are fairly stable and calm, it is instinct that says when a baby cries, the mom or dad finds out why the baby is crying and takes care of it. If the situation into which the baby is born is corrupted by drug or alcohol addiction, domestic violence, extreme poverty, or the parents have severe developmental disabilities or a mental illness, this cycle of need fulfillment can be inconsistent.

Attachment theorists explain that when the baby has a need and the caregiver meets the need, the newborn is able to trust that their environment is safe. During the first 18 months of life, the baby goes through the attachment cycle multiple times a day. They are hungry, they cry, they get fed, they stop crying. They are wet, they cry, they get a diaper change, they stop crying. They have gas, they cry, they are burped, they stop crying. Thirty, forty, fifty times a day they are getting the message that the world is a safe place and that other people can be trusted.

But a child who doesn't get that message as a newborn has a completely different view of the world. They have feelings like, "No one will take care of me" and "The world is a scary and dangerous place." They don't trust caregivers and they are often very angry and emotionally disturbed.

By now you are probably rolling your eyes and thinking, "If I would have wanted to buy a textbook about adoption I would have done so," but hang in there for a minute. Several adopted children have attachment issues in regards to their earthly parents, but I'm wondering about whether or not some of us may have attachment issues in regards to God.

Ideally, we could all experience God as He is: a loving and compassionate caregiver who wants nothing more than to nurture us and lovingly meet our needs. God has chosen His people, the church, to be His hands and feet and thus fallible broken people are left responsible to "be God" for us. And because of this -- not because of God's perfect nature -- I wonder if we might have some attachment issues when it comes to God.

Have you ever had negative experiences with a church, a pastor, or other Christians? Has a spiritual leader ever let you down? Have "godly" relatives shown a different side of God than makes sense? Those experiences may have transferred over to your feelings about God and whether or not He can be trusted.

Many times we are hurt by God's people. Someone says something that is repeated over coffee and we are stung with its venom. We spend years looking up to a spiritual leader who later is arrested for a financial or sexual crime. We attend church as a child where we are given a list of serious rules that must be followed, and our idea of God is not one of a gracious loving Father, but as a harsh judge with a gavel, ready to come down hard whenever we step out of line. A Sunday school teacher is needlessly critical. An uncle, the lay-leader at church, gets drunk at every family gathering. And as children, teens and young adults, we find ourselves concluding that because these people can't be trusted, neither can God.

Maybe I'm way off here, but I was conceived in a church building, literally -- my dad was the pastor of a storefront church and we lived in the upstairs apartment -- and I have been in church from my moment of conception until now, at age 47, nearly every Sunday of my life. I have been floored, disappointed, manipulated, hurt and completely shocked by the behavior of God's people. If so many of these things have happened to me, I am quite sure they have happened to you as well.

I can hear you saying, "OK, OK, I get your point, so what?"

Well, here's the deal. Kids with attachment issues take a very long time to come around. They need therapy, special parenting skills and time. And most of all they need parents who will be patient.

Ricardo is our tenth child to be adopted. By this time we had many children with attachment issues and we knew better than to try to force a child to be affectionate and connected to us; that each had to take their time. Ricardo was almost 10 when he arrived and had lived in several orphanages from the time he was less than a year old until he came home with us. He was definitely not interested in attaching to me as his mom. Interestingly, he had no trouble with my husband, Bart. I was the one he held at arm's length for a long time. I could hug him and he wouldn't fight back, but it took three years for me to get a kiss on the cheek and that was in a bribe situation. Smile.

But the day came, five and half years after he moved into my home, four and half years after he legally became my son, for him to initiate his first hug. Are you surprised to know it was one of the very best hugs of my life? But it had to come as a result of years of patience as I waited for him to return the love that I had been offering him unconditionally since day one.

I learned a lot during those five years about God's patient love. I watched an amazing little boy grow up right in my own home who I had claimed and dearly loved. I wanted him to return that love in some visible way, but for whatever reason, he couldn't do so. He had been hurt too many times in the past to open up and trust me. He was such an endearing kid -- extremely handsome, a brilliant sense of humor, and a talented athlete. And yet I knew I simply had to love him and wait.

God is like that. He loves you so much! He finds you beautiful and talented and fun and He wants to have an intimate relationship with you. He knows your past. He knows the pain you've experienced with His people and how it is keeping you from trusting Him. And He knows He can't rush you.

But He's there, waiting. Just as I reached out in small ways to Ricardo for years, God is reaching out for you. Look for Him in the world around you. Start to notice ways that He is coaxing you into a deeper relationship with Him. Pay attention to how He is showing you that He can be trusted.

Maybe there are parts of you that you are still withholding from God because of fear and you're not sure how long it will take for you to finally be able to trust Him. The good news is this: God's patience will outlast your fear. His patience will outlast your stubbornness. His patience will outlast your uncertainty, your insecurity, your anger and your pain. Though you may be tentative, He is waiting for you to take even the smallest step towards Him.

The 1981 movie "The Chosen" ends with this quote:

There is a story in the Talmud about a king who had a son who went astray. The son was told, Return to your father. The son replied that he could not. The king then sent a messenger to the son with the message... Come back to me as far as you can, and I will meet you the rest of the way.

That is our patient God. He beckons you to come as far as you can, and when you are ready to take that step, He'll meet you the rest of the way.

3

God's Stubborn Love

I spent the first 32 years of my life surrounded by people who understood that love is a give and take relationship. I always knew that there were things I did to make other people happy, and in return they did things to make me happy. We loved each other, right? I gave love, and I received love in return. It worked well. It made sense. It was neat and tidy and pleasant. And then I became a parent.

Just three months after our wedding we became foster parents to our first child, and within 5 years had acquired nine children. Because of genetics, prenatal exposure to alcohol and early years of abuse and neglect, these children had many diagnoses. To give you an idea of what we were facing, and to completely confuse you with terms you may have never heard, here is a list of the diagnoses at least one or more of our children has been given: Reactive Attachment Disorder, Bipolar Disorder, Fetal Alcohol Spectrum Disorder, Narcissistic Personality Disorder, Conduct Disorder, Obsessive Compulsive Disorder, Oppositional Defiant Disorder, Pervasive Development

Disorder, Post Traumatic Stress Disorder, Depression, Anxiety Disorder, PICA and Attention Deficit Hyperactivity Disorder.

Parenting children with these issues made love an uneven playing field. While some of our children are able to grasp the idea of love being a reciprocal relationship, others just don't seem to be able to participate in anything like it. They are very adept at the receiving part, but can't or won't give back. And frankly, this stinks. It doesn't feel good when I am taken advantage of or when days go by with no good feelings, words or actions coming from some of my children. However, I have to remember to ask myself if it is truly their fault.

Before I become completely caught up in whining, I recognize that this comes with the territory of parenting even children without issues. Very few women go to bed feeling completely appreciated by their kids. Have you ever cleaned a room to find it a complete mess an hour later? Ever assigned dishes to a 14-year-old and found the dishwasher loaded in such a way that not a single dish could ever get clean? Ever had a child forget your birthday or be especially mean on Mother's Day? Had the van door slammed by a teenage daughter after dropping her off at the mall one day when you were too busy to do so? Ever been yelled at, argued with, been told you were dumb? Ever felt that maybe the idea to have children wasn't such a great one after all? Do you ever end a day by titling that episode, "Children Behaving Badly"?

It is on days like this when I am especially in tune with what God must feel like being our Parent.

God has all kinds of children. He has those who give back sometimes and others who seem to ignore everything He does for them. He has those who understand what a reciprocal relationship is and those who are only takers. And yet, His love keeps coming. He isn't waiting around and expecting a response, or demanding one, or suggesting He might withhold His love if we don't give back. He just loves.

There are some days when I do a better job than others of being like God when it comes to my children. There are days when I can put my own needs away and focus on loving my kids -- even those who do not love me in return -- with a stubborn and persistent love. But there are days when I feel empty and cannot seem to find the strength to keep going.

It's those days when I am reminded of God's love for me the most. The days when I feel like I can't love unlovable people any longer are the days when God shows me that He loves ME regardless of my response to Him.

Do you ever take advantage of God's stubborn love? Do you accept the gifts He offers you daily without gratitude? Do you receive without giving back? Do you become angry and resentful towards Him when He is not the problem? Do you fight back when He reaches out?

We all do. We all have days when we are less than lovable. We have days when we are downright mean to God as He simply loves us. He invites us to be part of Him when we are most hateful.

It was 20 minutes before supper towards the end of a very long day. It seemed as though every child I called mine at that time was angry with me for one reason or another and I was exhausted.

Dominyk, the youngest at the time, came into the kitchen asking for something to eat because he was just so hungry he couldn't take it anymore.

"No honey," I said, in my most patient voice. "We'll be having supper in a little while."

"I HATE you!" he exclaimed.

Feeling as though most everyone did at that moment, I sighed, "Oh Dominyk, join the club."

"What?" he screamed incredulously, "I don't want to be in your club! I hate you!"

We have a God like that. A God who, when we come to Him with a heart full of hate, says, "Come join my club. I still love you, I still want you. I can handle your hatred and return it with my love."

As a teenager I found this quote, cut it out of a magazine and posted it on my bulletin board. I still think of it often because not only does it describe the way I should love others, but the way that God always loves us. I hope that its words find their way into the deepest part of your heart to reside there.

"I love you today, where you are and as you are. You do not have to be anything but what you are for me to love you. I love you now; not sometime when you are worthy, but today when you may need love most. I will not withhold my love, or withdraw it. There are no strings on my love, no price. I will not force it upon you when you are not ready. It is just there, freely offered, with both hands. Take what you want today. The more you take, the more there is. It is good if you can return love; but if you cannot today, that is all right too. Love is its own joy. Bless me by letting me love you today." (Author unknown).

God's Everlasting Peace

4

Calm in the Midst of the Storm

When I tell people that we have 12 children, I'm quite certain that what comes to mind for them is the food fight at breakfast in the movie "Cheaper by the Dozen." If you haven't seen the movie, it shouldn't take much imagination for you to picture what that might look like -- eggs flying through the air, lots of noise, the laughter, and the horrible mess everywhere that the movie never shows anyone cleaning up.

But in all actuality, life is never like that at our house. Unless it was mealtime or on Sunday morning before church, you probably wouldn't know that we have this many people living here. It's a pretty calm place a fair amount of the time. And because it is so quiet, we sometimes don't even know how many people are at home. Lately we have had what is most like a hospital census because at any given moment the number of people living here can change. Recently we had a week when the number of people sleeping here changed from 17 to six in 24 hours. With teenagers who either bring friends home or stay at friends' homes and two infant grandchildren and adult children coming and going, keeping track of who is here can require a degree in accounting.

In our family, as in most families that have two or more children, we have instigators and we have responders. Because we have far more than two children, we also have the audience. Who is the instigator, who is the responder, and who are those in the audience varies from day to day, but there are those who traditionally play one role or another based on their personality and special needs. And since we have incredibly effective instigators and very loud and willing responders, we can have moments of intense conflict.

Dominyk, who was our youngest for several years, is a classic responder. The combination of his special needs makes him very susceptible to the torture of his brothers. The joy that they receive from his reaction spurs them on and there are times when Dominyk just can't hold it together and he begins to rage. A tantrum, similar to that of a small child, comes pouring from his now man-sized body and the intensity of it can scare him.

On a good day, I can remain calm and not become emotionally entangled with his frenzied state. I can talk softly to him and encourage him to calm down. In fact, I have learned to use a phrase that has helped to settle him when he is at the end of himself. I take him into my arms and I say "Borrow from my calm."

I then slowly explain to him what that means. I calmly ask him to see if he can be quiet long enough to listen to my heart beating. I encourage him to try and match his heart beat with mine. I ask him to listen to my breathing and suggest that we breathe together. I hold him tightly and he clings to me and eventually he begins to mellow. His screaming stops. His breathing slows to match mine. And finally, his heart begins to beat as mine does.

Have you ever been in a situation where life seemed too out of control to handle? I'm not suggesting that you are having a raging screaming fit in front of your family -- though I confess to having done that on a few occasions. Maybe, like me, you have found yourself overwhelmed, lying in bed, covers over your head, the tears flowing so hard and they won't stop. Life is too chaotic. The challenges are too much to face. There is too much grief or struggle or pain to contain.

Maybe your struggle is with internal anxiety. Maybe it's not tears that overwhelm you, but fears. Outwardly your storm seems containable, but inwardly there are thoughts that run around your head like a train on a track, always circling back to the same things and they won't stop. Internally you feel chaotic and out of control.

I think you see where this is headed. There is a way to find peace in the midst of a storm, whether the hurricane be the chaos and struggle of the life outside of you, or the cacophony of voices screaming in your own head that will not be still. That peace can be found in the arms of God.

God invites you today to borrow from His calm. "Come", He says, as He wraps His loving arms around you. "Listen to my heart. Hear me breathing in your ear. Let me fill you with my peace."

Can you do that with me right now? Can you stop everything and run into God's arms for a tight hug? Can you match your breathing with the very breathe of God? Can you hear His heart enough to match your heartbeat with His? Can you feel, for this moment, His everlasting peace penetrating the chaos of your world?

It really is possible to have peace in the midst of the storm. We do so by "borrowing from the calm" of the Prince of Peace.

5

Peace Comes from Within

Are you one of those people who just can't not talk? That is so me! It takes a great deal of emotional energy for me to control my tongue. I have something to say about everything, and I cannot let an untruth float around in the air without correcting it. So, throw me and my big mouth into the mix with a bunch of children who love to argue, wouldn't know or care about the truth if it hit them in the face, and live for pushing my buttons, and you can imagine that there are very few quiet moments in our lives.

In addition to my mouth we have several other talkers at our house as well -- several other people who have even less impulse control than I. They like attention, they like to talk, they like to instigate, and they like to argue. I would say there are about six of us who do 90% of the talking in our home.

Two of the kids who do not fall into the "big mouth" category are Leon and Wilson. I wish you could meet them. They were the last to join our family at the ages of 12 and 8. They are Hmong by ethnicity but were raised in inner-city Dallas, Texas. They came to us at the end of some very difficult years with some of our older children, and we were shocked at their emotional health. We were used to dealing with many issues and these boys had none. We have often said that they have been our reward from God.

They are two of the calmest boys you will ever meet. They can be sitting in the midst of the chaos of our family and you can tell that their heart rates aren't increasing. They are so even-tempered and calm that simply looking at them can bring a smile to my face.

Bart and I have asked ourselves many times how it is that they can have such wonderful dispositions. Is it ethnicity? Is it genetics? Did their birth family, in spite of their addictions and illegal activities, provide them with a nurturing start? Was it their birth sister who cared for them as a very young girl? We have no idea how they lived through their early years and yet arrived at a place of incredible internal peace.

Wilson is a very small young man who is getting less and less happy about being called "little guy" or some derivative of that every day. But he also takes advantage of his size and allows himself to be quite spoiled by everyone around him. He's smart as a whip and has an incredible sense of humor.

Several months ago I called him peanut. He indignantly responded, "Peanut? PEANUT? How would you like it if I called you a semi?" I looked at him in mock confusion. "What in the world does a peanut have to do with a semi?" He just looked at me, shook his head and gave me that "you're so dumb" look, and walked away.

A couple of days later, out of the blue as we were driving somewhere in the van, he said, "Hey Mom, I'll make you a deal.

I really like almonds. So, if you'll call me almond instead of peanut, I'll downsize you to a mini-van."

Just a week before the writing of this chapter, Wilson was attending a training to become an acolyte (the person who lights candles in the front of the church). The woman doing the training told Bart that Wilson had really surprised her with his sense of humor. Weighing all of 70 pounds soaking wet, he had asked if he could try on the robe that the acolytes wear during the service. After he had it on, he turned to her and said, "Do you think this makes my butt look big?"

We are very entertained by Wilson's quiet sense of humor but there are days when I am sure he is troubled by all the arguing and noise that happens in our home, especially between Dominyk, Tony and I. Having been with us for the longest and having the most special needs, those two spend the day pushing my buttons and, being an uncontrollable talker, I simply respond, and respond, and respond. Wilson pulled me aside one day and said, "Mom. Did you ever think that the argument might be over if you stopped talking to them?"

A few days later five or six kids were surrounding us in our bedroom before bedtime. Tony and Dominyk were both in the room, arguing with each other and attempting to argue with me. Wilson was snuggled up with Bart on our bed and I was in the recliner. I looked at Wilson and winked, indicating that I was going to try his strategy. Tony and Dominyk were doing their best to get a response from me, and I just stopped talking.

However, the whole experiment wasn't working quite as planned. The more I ignored them, the more intense they became. I smiled at Wilson and he simply shook his head. A few minutes later he left his warm cuddle spot and crossed the room to climb into my lap, then took his small hands and put one over each of my ears. Looking into his beautiful face, I could feel the peace of this amazing little boy permeating my heart and mind.

Both Leon and Wilson are incredibly charming, gorgeous children who brighten our lives each day. They have taught me a great deal about what it means to have peace within and I am slowly learning that it is possible to focus on that peace and not be troubled by what is outside of myself.

But there is another problem. In addition to me having a big mouth, I have a mind that does not stop. I have often thought that if someone was allowed entrance into my internal world, they probably wouldn't stay long! They would probably be annoyed, frustrated and alarmed by my perpetual swirling thoughts and would undoubtedly be exhausted after only a few minutes of trying to live in there.

Do you have a mind like that? Do you have a brain that just won't stop churning? Even when my surroundings are calm and peaceful, my inner workings are not. They go and go and go, around and around and around, until I exhaust myself. Can you relate to that at all? Or am I just really weird? (Smile.)

Peace isn't just about finding calm from the storms that surround us, it is also about calming the storm within us. God's plan is to offer us the Prince of Peace who cannot only keep us from getting caught up in the chaos and struggle of the world around us, but who will still the raging thoughts in our minds and hearts.

One of my favorite verses is Psalm 46:10 where we are told, "Be still and know that I am God." God can probably be much gentler with some people and whispers, "Hush, my child." But with me sometimes, God has to say loudly and clearly, amidst all the voices in my head, "Would you just shut up for a minute?"

And He often says that to me when my mouth is not moving, but my internal voices are clamoring for attention.

Maybe today has been one of those days for you when your thoughts have been racing out of control and you have had no sense of peace. There has been no time for reflection or relaxation, meditation or renewal, and your mind is exhausting you.

Can you see God coming to you, placing His hands over your ears, and guiding your face so that it looks up into His? Can you hear Him either whispering "hush" or chuckling as He says, "Could you please just shut up for a minute?" Can you take time to breathe, to soak in His peace, and to enjoy His presence in your life?

Those of us who are talkers aren't going to suddenly wake up one day and be quiet, mild-mannered saints. Those of us who have minds that race all day long will not have the kind of personality change that we may want and be transformed into mellow, easy-going, relaxed people in days.

God created you the way you are -- He delights in the person He has made you to be. He also gives you the gift of Jesus, the Prince of Peace. This Jesus who simply said, "Peace, Be Still" and calmed the waves on the Sea of Galilee, can do the same in your heart and mind today. Philippians 4:7 tells us, *"And the peace of God, which transcends all understanding, will guard your hearts and your minds in Christ Jesus."*

Can you feel it? Can you sense His peace today? Then let it seep in to your frantic world, your bustling conversations, and your racing mind. Be still and know.

6

God's Peace is Already Ours

I have a few kids who do not see peace with me as something they are attempting to pursue. In fact, they seem to find pleasure in the opposite. They delight in pushing my buttons and getting me to respond in ways that aren't always a demonstration of my best self. Arguing is a sport to which they have committed themselves to becoming the Most Valuable Player.

In fact, most of my kids go through the stage where arguing seems to be the only thing they can do. If you are a parent of a preteen or early teen -- in fact, if you know a 12- or 13-year-old -- you know exactly what I'm talking about. The word "nu-uh" is a primary vocabulary word at that stage; arguments, especially with a parent who will participate, are their greatest joy.

I vividly remember a short trip around town with 6 kids in the van, 3 of whom were 13, one who was 12, one who was 11, and Wilson, the 9-year-old squeezed in somewhere. Wilson, our youngest and definitely smallest child, who is nearly always well-behaved and very soft-spoken, was trying to get my attention from his foot of space in the back seat that had been allotted to him by his siblings. "Mom, what time is it?" he struggled to ask over the din of noise.

I looked at the van clock rounded up the time and responded, "It's 2:30, Wilson." I suddenly heard a chorus of five voices saying, "Nu-uh! It's 2:28." Ah, the days of parenting three 13-year-olds. Who wouldn't want that?

It was during that time when I sometimes assigned the children my roles in arguing. For example, if Sadie would ask, "Can I spend the night at a friend's house on Saturday?" I would turn to Leon and say, "You love to argue so much, pretend to be me. You know all the answers to her questions. Just have the argument for me." And so I would sit back, listen to the two of them argue the issue, hear Leon present my case, and not have to engage my brain cells in an activity that really, for them, was nothing more than a hobby to pass the time.

Even though I have children who enjoy arguing, I also have a few who value peace with me as their mother. They remind me of myself at their age, because it was pretty important for me to not have my mom unhappy with me. But when these kids do disappoint me, I confess to being an imperfect parent and sometimes let them stew a bit, not offering a ready or easy resolution after their misbehavior.

Sometimes my kids want to make up really fast because they have an agenda and they know that if I'm mad I'm not going to let them to go a friend's house, or let them have a ride or whatever the case may be. During those times I drag things out. I wait for an authentic apology and I push them to check themselves and make sure that they are sorry even if I don't agree to give in to their next request.

The interesting thing is that I have already forgiven them before they apologized. I love my kids and they are teenagers.

They are going to make mistakes. They will mess up. One of them will do it today. Later they will apologize (most likely the next time they need something) and they will find that I have already forgiven them.

Every once in a while they don't believe me. They keep coming back to check and make sure that things are OK between us. Her conscience tender, and her relationship with us important to her, our youngest daughter has done this several times. A few weeks ago she came back to me to say sorry again and again during a busy day when I was harried and less attentive than I should be. Finally, late that night she came into my bedroom and said it one more time.

I said, "Sadie, its fine. I told you this morning that I have forgiven you. I told you this afternoon that I have forgiven you. It's not that big of a deal. I love you!" And she said, "But then why do I feel like you're still mad at me?"

Realizing what was really going on, I stopped everything and I pulled her into my arms and let her give me the real, connected, authentic apology she felt was necessary. I allowed her to cry a bit, and I told her yet again that I had forgiven her, and I sent her off to bed finally feeling peace with me.

But the interesting thing is this: she had that peace with me before she even apologized. The apology wasn't necessary for her to have my forgiveness and she certainly didn't need to say she was sorry multiple times. I had seen her heart, and this time her apology had not been about having her privileges restored. She was truly frustrated with herself for disappointing me and knowing that I had forgiven her was very important. She could not have that peace within herself until she could accept and believe that it had truly been offered.

How many times do we go through that routine with God? Maybe you feel like my kids do sometimes, and head to God with a request thinking, "Oh, great. There is no way God is going to give me that when I screwed up so badly. He's going to think I'm just saying I'm sorry because I want something."

You know what? God isn't an imperfect parent like me. He's not going to withdraw his peace from you and let you sit and stew and demand the right kind of apology in order to move on to the next thing. He is a perfect parent. He is sitting waiting for you to simply come to Him because the peace that He offers was already negotiated by Jesus.

Maybe the challenge is that you've done something huge. You know. One of those things, a really big sin in your mind that has distanced you from God and your heart is broken. Now when you want to talk to God, you feel like there is something that stands in your way from honestly communicating with Him. You move into His presence and the only thing on your mind is that one sin... that one mistake that haunts you. You have said that you are sorry many times, but you just don't feel peace.

Each time you come to Him you say that you are sorry again and God responds, "I have told you that I've forgiven you. It's not that big of a deal. I love you." And your response is? "Then why do I feel like you're still mad at me?"

Could it be that it's time for you to accept the fact that God has been at peace with you from the first "I'm sorry"? In fact, could it be that His peace was being extended to you immediately after the offense, even before the first "I'm sorry"?

Today is your day to let it go. Take a moment to head into God's presence just like Sadie came up to my bedroom a few weeks ago. It's OK to let God know that you still feel like He's mad at you. Let him wrap you into his arms and comfort you as you cry out your remorse again for that one thing... that big thing... that in your mind is unforgivable.

"But, Claudia," you might be saying to me. "I've done that before. I've already told God I'm sorry for that big thing a hundred times!"

Well, today things are different. Today you are going to believe God when He says that you now have peace with Him "through the Lord Jesus Christ" as Paul tells us in Romans 5.

Maybe the phrase "Make peace with God" has led us to believe that it takes a great deal of time and effort and action on our part. Really, it's just a matter of listening to Him speak His words of peace, forgiveness and reconciliation and acknowledging that His peace is ours -- before, during and after our sin.

Give yourself the freedom to accept that this is true. Forgive yourself so that you can feel the peace that has been there all along. Rest, relax and breathe in the peace that comes from God through Christ.

God's Infinite Wisdom

7

Guidance

I have a lot of teenagers. Way. Too. Many. But that goes without saying. Because I have so many, people often ask for my advice about parenting them. This might logically make sense to some, but assuming I know what I am doing because I have a lot of teenagers would be like assuming that someone knew a lot about dandelions simply because they were growing everywhere in their yard.

The following analogy sums up what it is like to parent teenagers. It is a word picture that explains quite clearly my current approach to raising teens.

Parenting teens is like teaching them to drive. They are in the driver's seat and you, as the parent, are in the passenger seat. You can give them all kinds of directions and ideas, discuss the law with them, explain tricky maneuvers, and riddle them with advice, but regardless of what you say, they are the ones in control.

Some parents refuse to let their kids drive their own lives as teens. They make all of their choices for them -- which may work well during the teen years but certainly doesn't prepare them for independent adulthood. Others spend so much time criticizing their kids' driving every time they are in the car with them, and giving so much advice, that eventually the kids take off in the car without them, regardless of whether or not they have a license. Wise parents sit in the front seat, bite their tongue, close their eyes if they must, and attempt to relax while the kids make mistakes.

And it usually goes like this:

Parent: "Um, you realize that if you turn left you're going to go into the ditch?"

Teen: "Shut up, I know what I'm doing. I know how to drive."

(Car heads into ditch.)

Teen: Oops. I guess I'm in the ditch.

Parent: "Well, this is certainly an interesting ditch. I'm sure glad there wasn't more damage to the car when we drove into it. How are you going to get out of the ditch?"

Teen: "I don't know. Can you help me get out?"

(At this point the parent intervenes and either instructs the child how to get out, letting them live with the natural consequences, or helps them out of the ditch momentarily, even driving if the teenager wants them to, until the car is back on the road).

Then, the next month, or maybe week, possibly later that same day...

Parent: "Um, you realize if you turn right you're going to go into the ditch?"

Teen: "Shut up, I know what I'm doing. I know how to drive."

(Car heads into ditch.)

Teen: "Uh, oh, we're in the ditch again. Can you help me get out?"

That pretty much sums up parenting kids from ages 13 to 23.

I spent most of the years parenting five of our six oldest children trying to do everything within my power to keep them out of ditches, accidents, etc., and it did not work. I occasionally grabbed the wheel and I spent far too much time talking to them about my expectations. Because of this they rebelled, went their own way, and now they are adults whose lives aren't turning out very well in most cases. With the remaining seven I've decided I'm just going to ride along. Sure, I'll give advice, sometimes when asked, and sometimes without request. I will not give permission for them to do something that I know is dangerous or wrong. The last thing I'm going to do is grab the wheel. It's pretty dangerous to fight for the steering wheel while the car is in motion.

When our youngest daughter (we have two) was 14 she got her first job at McDonalds and was being fairly responsible in that capacity. One day, when she was fifteen, she was very angry with me. And so to punish me she threatened to quit her job.

In the past, with her older sister, I would have said, "Oh, no you will not. Quit the job and I'll turn off the cell phone and ground you. You need to keep that job!"

I had learned a few things the first time around and I responded very differently. I said, "OK, if that's what you think is best. But you may not want to just quit by not going today. You should give two weeks' notice if you ever want to get another job. If you want to quit, that's cool, because I sometimes am busy when it's time to take you and it would save me some time."

I then said, "I'm getting ready to go to a meeting. You are supposed to be at work in 15 minutes. I will be in the van in 5 minutes. If you are there I will take you, and if not I'll assume you've quit." Four minutes later, there she was, in the van in uniform, complete with the little cap and on her way to work. It appears I've learned a few things over the years.

Parenting teenagers has given me a view of God's wisdom as He chooses not to grab my wheel. Sometimes I'm quite oppositional as I make my way through my day. I like to do things MY way and I don't want anyone telling me what to do. But He doesn't force Himself on me. He simply takes his place in the passenger seat.

Are you like that? Do you struggle with giving God control? Are you always able to give up the wheel, or do you often assign God the role of co-pilot, letting him ride along in the front seat? And do you hear him gently reminding you that if you go to the right you'll end up in the ditch?

Perhaps you are smiling in recognition of how you have done that and how well it has gone for you. Are you being reminded of a time where you looked up to God, sunk deep down in a ditch that He warned you about, saying, "Oops, God, it looks like I'm in a ditch. Can you help me get out?"

God is so wise. When we refuse to give up the wheel He is willing to patiently sit in the passenger seat of our lives. He doesn't stop loving us or guiding us or warning us. He still gives us calm instructions. In fact, Isaiah 30:21 even tells us, *"Whether you turn to the right or to the left, your ears will hear a voice behind you, saying, "This is the way; walk in it."* But through it all He knows that it is in our best interest is to let Him drive.

Lovingly, God goes through the same cycle of ditch exploration with us for a long time. He never forces us. He doesn't reach over and grab the wheel. He simply waits and invites us to conclude that He is the better driver and hand the wheel over to Him.

8

Justice

IT'S NOT FAIR!!!! Probably more than any other words (besides "knock it off" and "you're stupid") this phrase is repeated in our home over and over again, week after week, as our children demand justice.

But in our family justice is pretty tricky. Do you treat a child with an IQ of 68 the same as a child with an IQ of 118? Do you give the same responsibility to a child who has a healthy brain as to one whose brain cells were killed by alcohol in utero? Do you expect the same from a child who has known you since he was 9 months old as you do one who walked into your life at the age of 12?

One of the most interesting things is that the children who scream for justice are often the ones who get more than the others. Dominyk was our youngest for many years and has the very trying combination of ADHD and Obsessive Compulsive Disorder. For us, OCD has practically meant that our son has repetitive compulsive thoughts and ADHD means that everything in his head comes out of his mouth. The combination means that we as parents have some very long days.

But one of the things that Dominyk obsesses about is how things are not fair. Because of his persistence in asking and asking and asking for things, he often receives more than the other kids. He may get to go to the gas station with dad three times in one week, but the next day when another child goes for the first time in a month he screams, "NOT FAIR!"

The idea that those who scream the loudest for justice could be the ones who already have more was made clear to me when I spent two years as a lay missioner in Mexico before I was married. During that time we would host church services in remote villages with no running water, no transportation other than walking, and huts where families slept on a mat together on the floor. The irony, these people were more grateful and content than most of my friends in the United States. Here we are screaming "Not fair!" to God while there they were thrilled with everything they receive, grateful for even the smallest provisions of God.

Being a person who likes justice, I began my parenting journey trying my best to make everything fair. I had spreadsheets documenting expenditures, and tried to keep track of who had last had time alone with a parent, or how much we had spent on football cleats for the last kid. Then someone shared with me this thought:

"Fair does not mean that everyone gets the same thing. Fair means that everyone gets what they need."

That sentence has transformed my parenting. Having some compulsive tendencies of my own, it has taken a great deal of work to let go of my "spreadsheet" parenting, and now my kids are having their needs met in much healthier ways.

Do you remember the first time it hit you that you were going to have the same reward as the thief on the cross? I was a child or young teen and it just made me mad. What in the world was God thinking? I mean, seriously. Here I was, twelve or thirteen, and I was planning on spending my whole life doing all that I could to please God, and yet my reward was going to be heaven -- the same reward as that guy who met Jesus minutes before his death after being a very bad man.

IT'S NOT FAIR!!!!!

It's really not. In our view of fair being equal, it's not fair. But what if God's view of fairness isn't like ours? I don't want to rob from the impact of the chapters in this book that will talk about God's grace, but the bottom line is that we can't earn our reward anyway.

Even taking the discussion away from heaven and hell and eternal reward, what about bad things happening to good people or good things happening to bad people? What about brilliant and talented young people dying at age 17 while a whole bunch of unproductive people whom society views as losers seem to live to be 100? What about natural disasters that destroy countries? NOT FAIR.

What if God's perspective is different than ours? What if "Fair doesn't mean equal, it means that everyone gets what they need." What if God is the only one who TRULY knows what we need? If you and I truly believed this, how would it transform our lives?

Are you caught in a situation where you are perplexed by how unfair things seem? If so, take time today to view things from God's perspective. Understand that God's ways are not our ways and His thoughts are not our thoughts (Isaiah 55:9). Recognize that God is not only infinitely wise, but He is gracious, loving and kind. Trust him to do what is best.

A GLIMPSE OF GOD'S HEART

One of the most amazing people I have ever known is the late Bob Murphy, my pastor when I was in my late 20s. The recipient of a kidney transplant during his mid-20s caused many physical problems until he died at 45. He was one of the best preachers I have ever witnessed, a kind, gentle and patient man with a great sense of humor and a twinkle in his eye. He was also passionate about the things and people he cared about.

Knowing how gifted he was troubled me as I observed him struggling with various health issues. Why would God choose to let him suffer when he had so much to give? Why would his life be cut short when he obviously had so many plans and dreams to build God's kingdom?

Pastor Murphy didn't view life like that. In fact, one of his favorite quotes resonates in my head and heart often because not only did he believe it, he lived it. If anyone had reason to scream and shout "It's not fair" in God's face, it was a man who struggled with pain and illness year after year as he pastored churches, mentored young ministers, and was a caring and compassionate friend to those who knew him. Instead he quoted these words often:

God is, God Knows, God Cares
Nothing this thought can dim,
God always gives His best to those
who leave the choice with Him.

9

Telling Yourself the Truth

When we started our journey as a married couple we had big plans to do great things, foster care being one of them. We were going to reach into the lives of hurting children and help them, fix them even, and thus change our world. Fostering led to adopting and soon we had a houseful of kids. The problem was that they weren't getting fixed. In fact, some of them were having a harder time with life the older they became. We have experienced and continue to experience many difficult things.

I hesitate to mention them because I don't want to give you the wrong impression. I don't want you to conclude that we were really bad parents, which is sometimes the conclusion people draw. Nor do I want you to declare that we are saints, because we are certainly not that. Furthermore, I don't want you to think that I am trying to elicit pity, because the way that my journey has changed me is a true blessing.

My friend Kari tells me that reading my blog a few years back was like a bad car accident. You don't want to look but you can't help yourself. So maybe listing a few of our challenges will, if nothing else, make you feel better about your life. We all have to exist for some reason. Smile.

In our first 14 years of parenting we have been able to experience the following: psychiatric hospitalizations of two different children multiple times, teenage pregnancy, child protection investigations, three different children in juvenile detention and thus probation, two sons in adult jail (one in the state pen), false accusations by our children and even one therapist, having our lives threatened, and three of our children being placed outside of our home for various periods of time. I'm getting tired just writing this and remembering living through it!

In addition to the big things, there are also the daily things -- like being lied to, stolen from and disrespected, having parts of our home destroyed during tantrums, and being blamed for nearly everything that happens. Our lives have been turned upside down at times by the hatred and violence that exists inside children who have been unable to deal in the right ways with the pain inflicted on them by those who abused and neglected them. Hurt people hurt people. We understood this going in, but we didn't know how it would feel.

At this point you might be saying, "Hello? Is this the same author who has been telling us cute and funny stories, or did someone hijack Claudia's keyboard?" How could a person who has been through all this be cracking jokes and writing a book that is typically so upbeat and positive?

Wow, am I glad you asked that question! In this chapter I will tell you how we have survived the things we have encountered so far and are still smiling (most of the time). Ready? Here it is. We have trusted in God's wisdom and told ourselves the truth. Consistently reminding ourselves of God's truth found in Scripture and revealed to us daily has helped us through every situation. It is borrowing from God's wisdom in order to tell ourselves the truth.

Each of us needs a collection of truths that we can repeat to ourselves to help us through the hard days. I will give you a sample of some of the truths that have helped me during the last several years.

1) God doesn't call the equipped, He equips the called. Of course I'm not the person who came up with that phrase, but at the center of it is an important truth. He called me to do this. Because He called me, He will not leave me halfway through the journey and let me fend for myself. He will give me everything that I need to make it through the life that He has called me to live.

What's your struggle today? Are you facing some hard times causing you to wonder whether or not you are cut out for the life you've been given? It's time to tell yourself the truth. God called you and He will be faithful to see you through. No exceptions.

"But what if He didn't call me to this but I somehow got myself into it?" you may respond. One of my favorite verses in the Bible has always been Romans 3:3, asking the question of whether or not our lack of faith will nullify God's faithfulness, because I think we ask ourselves that question all the time. If I mess up and don't do the right thing, does that mean that God is going to back out of the deal? Paul responds in the next verse, "Not at all!" There is your answer. God is faithful to see you through every situation, even those that He didn't necessarily call you to enter.

2) It's not my fault. This truth is incredibly important in dealing with difficult people, especially those who are battling mental illness. Self-differentiation is the idea that you can

separate yourself from other people emotionally and not have emotional health dependent on other people. It means that you can recognize which parts of the problem you have created and address those without letting yourself take on the issues of those around you.

Several of our children blame us for every bad decision they have ever made, especially those, ironically enough, that we had specifically warned them about. In these situations I have to constantly tell myself the truth. It's not my fault. I didn't cause this problem and I'm not going to carry the blame for it.

Do you find yourself taking on the blame for other's choices? Stop it. Tell yourself the truth about the situation they are in and recognize only the part you played in it. Don't carry the burden of another's addiction, or mental illness or misbehavior. Do a quick self-exam and fix those things that are your responsibility and then let it go.

3) It's not about me. I have had to remind myself of this every day as a parent, wife and friend. The moment that I begin to focus on myself and why things aren't going my way is the moment things start to unravel. Feelings like irritation, frustration, annoyance, bitterness and resentment begin to trickle in and they slowly poison me until my heart starts to harden.

I am not advocating a mindset that says that I am not worth any of my own attention or that taking care of me is not important. I am saying that recognizing that it isn't all about me keeps my head on straight.

Most of us put others first naturally as a result of our love for them. We might give a piggy back ride to a toddler even if our back hurts, or a ride to a teenager even though we have a deadline on a project. We cook meals when we have upset stomachs and don't feel like eating. We attend band concerts of

7th graders whose instruments are screeching with errors and smile and clap even though on the inside (which we would never confess to anyone) we are bored senseless after the third number and the music has given us a headache. This is what we do because we love our kids.

When we begin to focus on ourselves life becomes an incredible burden. When we begin to perform acts of love from another part of us they become acts of duty or acts of fear (if I don't do this, will my family leave me?). At this turning point, when what we do stops being about our love for others, and we start to dwell on our own needs, we start to lose our ability to cope.

If your focus is a bit off today, it's easy to realign it. Remind yourself that love is selfless. It's not about you. Love is about giving without expecting to receive in return. C.S. Lewis taught that we should not wait until we felt like loving before we began to act lovingly, because the loving acts would bring about loving feelings. Try it sometime and see if it doesn't turn things around.

4) Something that I often tell myself is that in the light of eternity, this isn't going to matter all that much. In fact, in five years it isn't going to matter. With some of my petty thoughts, I may not remember this crisis a week from now. I'm not a worrier -- I have a husband who is excellent at that so I just let him worry for the whole family -- but I do tend to dwell on certain things, typically things that aren't going to matter much in the long run.

5) I am dearly loved by God. Colossians 3:12 tells us, "*As God's chosen people, holy and dearly loved....*" Wow. God loves me! He's crazy about me. No matter what I've done or what I will do He doesn't stop loving me. He delights in me! He accepts me for who I am and He always will.

That truth seems to be a constant theme in my life lately and I tell myself often. God's love for me is complete and it is enough. He can see me through any situation. His love sustains me and fills me and keeps me going. I can celebrate His love today.

These five statements are samplings of truths I must tell myself every day. There must be dozens of sentences that I repeat in my mind as I am daily living through one challenge after another. The truths found in Scripture that were ingrained in me from childhood come back and repeat themselves in my head.

I have a challenge for you today. Take out a piece of paper and put it somewhere where you can find it easily. On the top of the paper put the words "Tell yourself the truth." When you are reading the Bible or other helpful books or as you are living through your day, jot down sentences that are true, similar to the examples above.

Then over the next few weeks when you start to feel overwhelmed, go back and pick up that piece of paper and read through it. Let the truths of God's word and your own experience over the years speak back to you and you'll make it through whatever challenge you're facing.

Seek God's wisdom and tell yourself the truth.

God's Abundant Joy

10

Make Room for Joy

Jesus tells us in John 10:10: *I have come that they may have life, and have it to the full.* He wants our lives to be abundant and overflowing with good things. He not only wants us to notice the good God has done for us but He wants us to celebrate it wholeheartedly.

Of all of our 12 children, John was the one most excited about being adopted. There were several complications surrounding our visit to meet him and his two birth sisters and they had been looking forward for weeks to meeting us. At the last minute they were told that we wouldn't be able to come after all. They didn't know it, but at the last minute things worked out and we were able to arrive just two hours after they had expected us.

Ages 8, 6, and 4 at the time, they were quietly in the back family room watching a movie with their foster siblings when we arrived. We made our way back to where they were sitting and when John saw us and recognized us from our picture he literally ran across the room and jumped into our arms. The joy on his face was something I'll never forget. His little heart was overwhelmed with the idea that he would have a mom and dad to call his own.

Children are much better at making room for joy than we are. As I listened to a keynote speaker at a foster care conference, a man who has been working with foster and adopted children for over 30 years, I was surprised to learn that children can only experience one emotion at a time. Many times children who have been abused or neglected can only focus on the anger that is within them. But John, in January of 1999, was focusing on joy.

John had some pretty hard things happen to him during his first eight years of life and, as he grew up in our home, some of the negative emotions as a result came to the surface, leading him to a very difficult adolescence. That moment when he was eight and we came walking into that foster home, his heart was only full of joy. There was no room for anger, unforgiveness, or resentment to live because there was too much joy.

I wonder if maybe that is my problem sometimes. What if my heart can only hold so much and that space is so clouded up by negative emotions that there is no room left for joy? If that's the case, it's time for me to clean it out and make room for joy.

I've never been an angry person by nature. When I was growing up there were only two people in the entire world who could make me angry -- my two younger brothers. They knew exactly how to push my buttons and make me see red! I had homicidal thoughts as a child when they would tease me mercilessly.

But after I grew up and moved away from home I can count how many times I was angry in 14 years on one hand. And then I got married and started to acquire children. In fact I started to acquire children who were as invested in pushing my buttons as my brothers had been and I found myself battling anger once again. My children's behaviors and actions pushed me farther and farther down the road that started with anger and led to unforgiveness, bitterness, and resentment.

Sometimes admitting to ourselves that we have an anger problem isn't easy. Maybe anger is disguised as something else and you don't recognize it. Maybe, like me in my single, childless days, you don't have a lot of triggers and have remained anger-free. But if you are a person who is recognizing that anger is the thing that is filling your heart, leaving no room for joy, then this chapter is for you. It is time to make a plan to walk away from anger and clear out some space for joy.

One of the tricky things about anger is that it is an emotion that can't be controlled. Your response might now be, "What are you talking about? Didn't you just say I needed to get rid of it? How can I do that if it can't be controlled?"

I'm glad you asked.

Anger is an emotion and during the first 30-60 seconds it is simply there. That's why Paul says in Ephesians 4:26: "*In your anger do not sin*" ... because everyone is going to get angry. That's a given. The issue is not the anger, but the thoughts and actions that we choose after the emotion that either lead us to sin or to victory over it.

Let me use a simple example. Have you ever stepped on a Lego™? I have and it HURTS. When I step on a Lego™ my first emotion is anger and my first thought is "I am going to have to kill whoever put that Lego™ on the floor." Now of course, I don't carry out my murderous thoughts. In fact, I calm myself down and remind myself that I am not going to harm anyone.

We all have what some psychologists call "flash anger," that sudden emotion that overwhelms us. What we do with it is the key. We can process it, forgive the offender, forget about it and move on, or we can let it build.

One of the Alcoholics Anonymous sayings is "*Resentment is a cup of poison I drink hoping the other person will die.*" Breeding resentment and unforgiveness doesn't harm anyone but our self. It's a trap that leads us to a slow painful death instead.

If I had to list my greatest challenge in the past three years, it would be battling resentment. Our efforts to create an environment where our children feel loved unconditionally often leads them to expect too much from us or to take advantage of us. As they have grown older and made bad choices, my resentment grows as they ask us time and time again to bail them out (sometimes literally) of tough situations.

As I mentioned in the introduction to this book, this past summer we came to the conclusion as a couple that life wasn't going to turn out quite like we had planned. An empty nest now seems like a fantasy. Employed adult children are falling into the same category. The "children grow up, get married, and then give us grandchildren" plan isn't exactly how it is turning out. For a few months I found myself battling resentment as I wanted to scream at God, "We didn't know we were signing up for this!"

I found out during those months that I am the one who gets to decide whether I remain resentful, angry and bitter or if I have a heart that is full of joy. I can shove God out of my thinking and ignore the gifts He gives me. I can focus on the negative and ignore the positive. Or I can turn things around by turning to God and asking Him to remove my spirit of unforgiveness and bitterness and replace it with his joy.

MAKE ROOM FOR JOY

Is it time to forgive and move on? Have you been holding on to something very tightly that you need to let go? Are you realizing that the resentment and unforgiveness you harbor in your heart is turning into poison that is slowly killing your spirit? Wouldn't you like to replace it with joy? Today can be the day.

It's time to do a little housecleaning. Forgive someone. Make a decision not to harbor negative thoughts, asking God to help you change your thinking. Surround yourself with joyous happy people. Consciously change your negative thoughts and replace them with positive ones. Put reminders up in your house of positive scripture verses or better yet, memorize them! Listen to upbeat positive music. Begin to focus on the good.

When you find God's spirit emptying of all the junk, celebrate the joy that makes its way in to take up all that space. There's more room in there than you think!

11

Joy in Unexpected Places

Every family has legends... stories that are told and retold when company comes or when a new person joins the family. It might be an embarrassing moment or some clever thing a member of the family did when he was three years old. Possibly it is a vacation or special occasion that was packed full of awesome things, and retelling it brings back memories that evoke the same emotions as the event itself.

In our family, we have much material for embarrassing moments, clever comments, and special occasions (we have nine birthdays between Nov. 4 and Dec. 29!) But it is interesting to me that some of our kids' favorite memories involve fairly serious things -- situations that would definitely be placed in a category with a title something other than joy.

If you came to our house and I, the designated family entertainer, was called upon by one of my children to tell stories, you would most likely hear the request, "Mom, mom. Tell the knife story! You know, where John pulled the knife on you?"

Upon hearing this you would undoubtedly become quite shocked and wonder what in the world could be funny about that!

I really don't think I'm going to get away with not telling you the knife story right now, so here goes...

When Jimmy arrived from Guatemala he learned English quickly because he loves to talk. He didn't master the language before he started using it... a lot. And since he loves drama of any kind, he was quick to tell stories about what was happening at home to anyone who would listen.

One morning when John was about 12, he was having a particularly hard start to his day and since curbing his aggression was something he struggled with during those years he didn't respond appropriately. He grabbed a knife and headed toward me, but I knew that he wasn't going to stab me and so I calmly said, "John, give me the knife," and within a few seconds the entire scene was over. He ran out the door and ran to school where the kids were going to have breakfast.

As his younger brothers and sisters headed to the elementary school, I suggested that they may not want to sit by John as he was pretty upset. I encouraged them to give him some time to calm down and sit somewhere else.

Jimmy could barely contain his excitement about this event when he arrived at school and so he told the breakfast ladies, using his not-yet-perfect English to recount the morning, "My mom say no sit by John. He have a very big knife!"

The women, of course, were very alarmed by this and contacted the administration about this issue. I can just hear them talking about that "crazy Mrs. Fletcher" who sent her kid to school knowing he had a knife, but warning only his siblings. Of course, we cleared the understanding quickly and the event simply lives on as a hilarious legend of our strange yet wonderful family.

Another example of our unique version of normal is the ways that Bart and I try to scoop each other for really good blog material. For a period of time we were both blogging quite a bit and it was important for us to relay a less than pleasant event first and in a most clever way. This caused us to look at our situations very differently.

Our kids don't break the law on Friday night because their father is a pastor. Thus Saturday night, since their dad has to get up and preach the next day, has become their crime night of choice. But one night we hit the jackpot.

Do you know anyone who can say that they have had the same vehicle stolen on the same night in two different counties by two of their own children? Well, now you do. And as we were sitting at 3 a.m. at one police station while the two counties argued about who was going to press charges against which child, we were actually cracking up. We were joking about who would blog first, how we would tell the story and how many hits it would bring to our blog.

Now granted, you may not have these kinds of stories to tell, but if you look back at some of your funniest moments, have they not been in the midst of a difficult situation? Have you not been able to see glimpses of joy through pain?

As human beings I believe we try to separate our lives into categories. If I gave the following list to a fifth grader, she would have no trouble making two lists -- joys and sorrows or good things and bad things -- and quickly put them into one or another: birthdays, hospitalizations, funerals, anniversaries, vacations, cancer, weddings, unemployment, the circus, Chuck-

E-Cheese, car accidents, amusement parks, broken bones, graduation day and divorce.

It is relatively easy to put these events into categories. Hospitalizations, funerals, cancer, unemployment, car accidents, broken bones and divorce are obviously "sorrows" or bad things. Birthdays, anniversaries, vacations, weddings, the circus, and amusement parks are all joys or good things. Chuck-E-Cheese? It's a joy if you're a kid but if you're a parent, not so much.

Really, each of the events has a mix of joy and sorrow. If we allow ourselves to admit it, there are sad times during the happiest of events. We can have negative emotions during even the "best of times." The opposite can also be true. In the midst of some of life's most difficult events we can see glimpses of joy if we look for them.

Edwin Marckum said, "*Defeat may serve as well as victory to shake the soul and let the glory out.*" Could it also be that pain and sorrow as well as happiness can shake us a bit and let the glory of God show forth? Doesn't he sometimes reach out to us from the most unexpected places with bits of joy?

Granted, your life is probably not much like ours, and that's good! I know you can think back to the last thing in your life that goes on the "sorrow" list and see some glimpses of joy in the midst of it all. Maybe a hospitalization allowed for some really good time to visit with an old friend. Or maybe something happened at a funeral that caused so much laughter that the story will be retold for generations. Maybe you have felt God's joy peeking through one of your darkest days through an unexpected beautiful sunset, or the arrival of a bird at your window, or a rainbow after a horrible storm.

God's like that. He shows up with some joy when we least expect it. Sometimes His joy bursts into our lives with a sudden overwhelming emotion and other times He simply sneaks in and plants a small seed that begins to grow. Our job is to be open to the possibility that God just might surprise us with joy in the most unexpected places.

One of my favorite hymns, O Love that Will Not Let Me Go, by George Matheson says it best:

Oh Joy that seekest me through pain,
I cannot close my heart to thee;
I trace the rainbow through the rain
And feel thy promise is not vain
"That morn' shall tearless be"

12

Joy Comes from Gratitude

In the city where we live the school district has determined that if you live less than two miles away from the school you do not qualify for free bus service. We live 1.7 miles from the junior high and high school and thus we give our kids a ride to school. There are other kids in our neighborhood who, due to parent schedules and other factors, must walk or ride their bikes. My kids, however, have their own private ride in a limo by their own private chauffeur, otherwise known as mom and the minivan.

A couple years ago I had three kids who found it funny to not speak to me at all on the way to school. Relieved to have their lives cleared of the noise of their louder siblings who had been dropped off already, they would shut down and not say a word. As the kids get dropped off I say to them every day, “Have a great day. I love you. Don’t miss me too much. Make good choices and remember, every day counts.” And some days I even add, “It’s a great day to be a Fletcher!”

Their response? Stone silence. Every day.

On our route to school at that time there was a young lady who is a refugee from Sudan. A victim of polio, one leg is much shorter than the other and she uses crutches. The school is about 8 blocks from her home and she walks. It bothered me when it was nice out, but in a blizzard when it was bitter cold it drove me crazy to see that nobody was offering to pick her up. How many people drove by her every day and didn't check into it? I determined to do something about it.

Every day as we walked by her I became increasingly angry and spewed about it to my silent children until finally I let them have it. I explained to them that I didn't have to give them a ride -- they could walk like many other people. I mentioned that their lack of gratitude drove me crazy when there were others, like the girl with the crutches, who had to walk. I let them know that unless things changed and they could at least say thank you as I dropped them off, I would be dropping them off at the corner and they could walk the remaining 8 blocks to school. I explained that this would be the last time there would be silence in the van when I dropped them off. They needed to practice being grateful.

There are two "rest of the stories" to this account. One of them is that a few days later I happened to be at the school for a conference and met the "girl with the crutches." She and a bunch of her friends were stuck at school without a ride. I offered to give them one and before I dropped her off, I gave her my number and told her to call me any time she wanted a ride. Throughout that winter, whenever she called, we picked her up and took her to school.

In addition, my kids started to develop the habit of gratitude. Not about everything, and not willingly, but about this one thing -- a ride to school -- they said thank you. It's been two years since this started and we never see the "girl with the crutches" anymore, but when I drop my kids off for school now I hear a chorus of thank you's And our morning drives have lightened up a little and we have a bit more fun. Somberness has been replaced with what could almost be defined as joy (if teenagers can experience that feeling before 10 a.m.).

One of the ways I have made it through very difficult times during the past several years has been to look for one thing each day to be thankful for. I call them "moments of joy." I look for one thing that has made me smile or feel good inside. It could be a hug or a kiss from a child, an almost smile from a newborn grandchild, a funny thing that happened, special time away for lunch with my husband... whatever it is... I remember it.

On the nights that follow my hardest days, I look back and find that "moment of joy." I tell myself that if there is only one, it's enough to have lived the day for. Furthermore, I remind myself that it is worth getting up the next day to discover what moment of joy will peek its head through my current situation and surprise me. One moment of joy each day is all I need and if I look for it I always find it.

We don't have a God that forces us say thank you like I have done with my kids. He provides us with so much and wants us to notice. He wants us to develop habits of gratitude -- not because He needs us to say thank you, but because we need to experience the joy that stems from gratitude.

During some of the toughest times in my life I have challenged myself to write a gratitude list. It always puts things into perspective. I put the list on my blog as a reminder to myself and others that we need to be grateful. Here was my list on Sept. 8, 2010:

1) All of our 12 children, and their significant others, and our grandchildren, one born, and one unborn, are healthy.

2) There have been no major episodes of aggression in our house all week. (OK, now putting that in writing is just inviting trouble, but hey, wait, this is a gratitude post.)

3) I have an amazing husband who does way more than most husbands do and then steps in whenever things are hard for me or I'm feeling down and does even more.

4) I have a few really good friends in our town and in our church that put up with me, even when I'm just not quite like everyone else.

5) I have a great team of online friends who support me by their writing, their blogs, their comments, their emails, offering all kinds of encouraging words to read daily.

6) I have more than enough food to eat, clean water to use and drink that I don't have to haul, a place to sleep that is temperature controlled, several choices of clothing to wear each morning -- and those things combined have me living in the top 10% of the world's population for sure.

7) I am living my dream of speaking and writing, even if it isn't full time.

8) I have jobs that allow me to make a difference in the world doing something that I love AND get paid for it.

9) I have incredible parents who have loved me, nurtured me, prayed for me and offered their support for all of my near 47 years.

10) I have a God who is awesome, amazing, personal, and who has the power to do ANYTHING. He has given me the gift

of His grace and He never lets me down. He is always there to catch me when I'm falling and set me back on a firm place so I can keep going.

Just like my kids have become more grateful because they have been forced to practice the habit of gratitude, my gratitude journal does the same for me. As I articulate each thing for which I am grateful, I notice more and more things. In addition, I have found that after writing a gratitude post, joy can't help but sneak in. I find myself beginning to celebrate the things for which I am grateful and God shows up with his abundant joy.

Don't think it's true? Try it. Sit at your computer or pull out a sheet of paper and just write down five things for which you are grateful. You may find yourself not able to stop at five -- or to not be able to choose which five to jot down. It's my guess that as you begin to write, joy will start to filter in.

I'm convinced that God is always faithful to provide us with at least one moment of joy for each day. The trick is we have to look for it. Look back on your last 24 hours. Where was your moment of joy? If you look for it, you'll find it. Give it a try.

God’s Amazing Grace

13

Acceptance

Jimmy is a trip. He is a gregarious, funny, now adult whose lower IQ is compensated for by his great sense of humor and his desire to please. When we were approached about adopting him 9 years ago this fall, we were told that the orphanage had been around for 25 years and had been run by the same two women who declared that he was the naughtiest boy they had ever had in all their years there.

I like to tell people that when Jimmy showed up here it was his full intention to be the naughtiest kid in our house as well, but within weeks he had sized up his competition and realized that he didn't have a chance so he settled right in. He can still be described, now almost 19 years old, as naughty. His behavior drives some of his teachers crazy and can cause us to have a strong desire to pull our hair out at times, but most of the time he is delightful.

Jimmy loves to talk, and as he has learned English the very funny things he has said have become family legends. From his first night at our dinner table where he mispronounced fish sticks several times much to the delight of his siblings up until a month ago when he uttered the sentence, "I'm just being sarcasm, for FYI," his attempts to master English have provided us with a great deal of laughter.

But underneath all the naughtiness, Jimmy has an intense desire to please. He tells everyone that he is the "best cleaner" of anyone in the family and he really is. The fact that he hides or throws things away that he isn't sure what to do with is a bit difficult to deal with at times, but when he is finished cleaning a room it is CLEAN. And as soon as he is finished he comes to find me saying, "Hey mom. Do you want to come and see?" So whether it is the garage or the kitchen or the bathroom, he wants me to come inspect his work and is delighted when I approve of what he has done.

I love it when he tries hard to please me. It makes me feel good to know that he loves me enough to want to make me happy. I love to see his sense of satisfaction in a job well done. I love to see his pride and the smile on his face. But you know what? The fact that he did a great job on the garage doesn't make me love him more than I already do. In fact, I couldn't love him more than I have since the day I claimed him as my son.

This fall my husband has been preaching about grace, and he pointed out something that I have never heard before. According to my calculations, I have heard approximately 8140 sermons in my life. (Yes, I did use a calculator to figure this out.) I don't remember this thought ever crossing my mind. God said the words, "*You are my Son, whom I love; with you I am well pleased.*" (Luke 3:22) before Jesus did ANYTHING. He hadn't performed a miracle yet, hadn't spoken a word of teaching, hadn't done a single thing in his adult life that God would be pleased about. God accepted Jesus before he achieved anything.

In his preaching, Bart explained the cycle of grace and the cycle of works Dr. Frank Lake introduced. Dr. Lake suggested that the cycle of grace begins with God's acceptance of us, leads us to finding substance in God, which brings about our sense of value, and allows us then to achieve. Our society, however, approaches things from the opposite direction. We start with our achievement, which is where we define our value. That leads us to find sustenance in things and other people instead of God, and we eventually are able to find a cheap form of acceptance in the people around us.

You may want to read that paragraph through a few times, because it's good stuff!

I was fortunate enough to have parents that were able to demonstrate to me the powerful concept of God's acceptance of me. They were very committed to developing my self-image and helping me to see myself as God sees me. In fact, I tease them sometimes for over-doing the self-concept stuff. I remember being in junior high, by far the ugliest kid in the class, and having very few friends.

OK, now I need to stop for a minute. I'm sure you are thinking "Oh sure, we all felt like the ugliest kid in junior high." Listen, I have pictures. I have proof. If you looked at them, you'd agree with me. But I digress.

I remember coming home from school in 7th grade and saying to my mom, "Nobody at school likes me." And she would say, "Wow! That's weird. I wonder what's wrong with them?" While that did wonderful things for my self-image, it probably isn't the best approach as an adult. I still find myself thinking when someone mentions that they have heard so-and-so doesn't like me, "Wow, I wonder what's wrong with them?"

Looking at my life, however, I have met so many people who really don't understand this concept of God's acceptance of them. It usually stems from their childhood where a parent or important person in their life was overbearing or critical or demanding and they internalized the idea that they were not quite good enough. They started to believe the lie that love is conditional -- it is based on performance. They have spent their lives attempting to earn that feeling of acceptance by doing things as perfectly as they can.

Somehow in the process of all this, they become trapped. They tell themselves that what they do, rather than who they are, is the core of their relationships with other people, even those closest to them. This intense desire to please others makes them great people to live with, be friends with, and hang with. I do not get the impression that it makes them feel very happy or content. They are caught in a cycle of doing their very best to please others, but they never feel like they measure up.

I hope that you, like me, have a few people in your life that truly do love you for who you are and don't have expectations that your behavior or achievement have to measure up to some minimum standards in order for them to love you. When I am with those treasured folks in my world, I have the freedom to simply be me. I know that nothing that I do could make them love me more than they already do.

Are you one of those people trapped inside a cycle of attempting to perfectly please those around you? Are you ensnared by the lie that you are not good enough if you don't perform up to others' expectations? Do you find yourself working intensely to gain approval in all areas of your life?

If that is you, possibly you are making the same mistake with God. Perhaps you have expectations you've placed upon yourself that lead you to believe that God will not be pleased with you unless you do things right, and nothing that you do ever seems quite right.

God likes it when you attempt to please Him! He is thrilled that you love Him enough that you want to make Him happy. He likes to see the pride you have and the way it makes YOU feel when you have a sense of satisfaction in a job well done.

Guess what? The fact that you did a great job doesn't make Him love you more than He already does. Nothing you could do could make Him love you more than He has since the day he created you.

I wonder if this, more than anything else, is the message that God wants us to completely understand. His heart is so full of love for us and He wants us to know that his love doesn't have anything to do with our actions or our performance or how well we do something.

God loves you because you are YOU. He loves the things inside of you that make you the person you are and the person He created you to be.

If you have been trapped in the cycle of performance and perfectionism, it is my prayer that this will be a holy moment for you. Hear God as He pulls you into a tight embrace and whispers these words to you:

You are mine. I created you to be just as you are and I love you with all my heart for who you are, not for what you do. There is nothing you can do to make me love you any more than I have loved you since the day you were conceived. There is nothing you can do to make me love you any less. Relax. Rest in me. Let my grace and my acceptance transform you as you finally allow yourself to believe that you are perfect in my eyes through Christ regardless of the imperfect things you do. Allow yourself to be free of your need to do and simply be the amazing person you are. Cuddle up in my everlasting arms and celebrate the unique and priceless treasure that I created you to be. You are my beloved child and in you I am well pleased.

14

Erring on the Side of Grace

Have you ever had a really good pity party for yourself? I mean the kind where you feel mistreated, unappreciated, or even invisible? I have them sometimes and they come out of nowhere. But they usually happen after "the last straw."

The last straw could be something like:

* Finding 6 pairs of shoes in the garage, three of them belonging to the same child (when they belong only inches away from where they have been flung);

* Clearing my schedule to make sure that one of the kids has exactly what they need for something special, and then being treated disrespectfully during the entire event;

* Discovering chips and salsa in the living room, where nobody is supposed to eat, for the fourth time in a week, spilled and seeping into the sofa pillows;

* Getting a text in the middle of a stressful work day informing me that the latest crisis in my daughter's life is somehow entirely my fault;

* Realizing after I've uttered words that I can't take back, that the stress in my life has come to the point where I am taking it out on the one person who doesn't deserve it: my incredible husband;

* Working my hardest on a project for one of my jobs and then being told that the plan has changed and that the project is no longer necessary;

* Arriving at my third airport of the day to discover that my bags will not be arriving until the next day;

* Having an adult child come to my home with a grandchild and not even bothering to let me know they are stopping by, so that I miss out on baby time.

Now, any of those things, one at a time, might not be that big of a deal. But when they come at the same time, one of them can be the last straw.

And then it's time for my party. I may slam around, muttering under my breath about how no one in the entire family is capable of replacing an empty toilet paper roll. I might sit staring into space asking myself questions like, "Has it really come to this? Is this all there is? Will my life never be better than this?" I may simply crawl under my covers and have a good cry.

And then I start to plot my revenge. Maybe so-and-so doesn't need three pairs of shoes if they are just going to leave them everywhere. Maybe the next time we go shopping, no shoes for him. How about that big special event? Next time that kid has one, they are WALKING to the store to buy their own cupcakes. What about texting? It's being turned off, TODAY. Oh yeah, no more chips and salsa, EVER. This family will never eat another tortilla chip as long as I live.

I let my mind spin into all kinds of ways that I will punish and consequence and withdraw from and torture these PEOPLE who have DESTROYED my life. OK, OK, so when I finally have a pity party, I make sure it's a good one.

After I calm down and express some of these plans of revenge to my ever-so-patient husband, he reminds me of his philosophy when it comes to our children. He says, "I always try to err on the side of grace."

What a way to ruin a good pity party!

All of us who are parents -- or friends -- or wives -- or sisters -- or daughters -- have decisions to make about whether or not to distribute justice or to offer grace and mercy. And it's not always easy to find balance.

At the beginning of our parenting journey we applied many consequences and everyone earned every penny we spent on them. We wanted to teach them about real life and how there was no such thing as a free ride. We were consistent in making sure that we were not spoiling our kids and that they would learn lessons that would prepare them to live in the real world.

After practicing this for some time, we realized that some of our kids were never going anywhere with those guidelines. They didn't understand consequences and were so scattered that they really could not earn money very well. Periodically we would schedule what we called "Grace and Mercy Day."

On each of these days we talked to our kids about how we defined those words. We shared with them that grace is getting what you don't deserve while mercy is not getting what you do deserve. We talked about how their behavior that week had been bad and they deserved to be punished. Today we were not going to give them what they deserved. They were not going to be grounded nor have their privileges taken away for the offenses of the week before because that day was a day for mercy.

We explained to them that they would be receiving something they didn't deserve. We told them about God's grace and how grace means that we receive things from God that we cannot earn. On that particular day they were going to be given something that they did not deserve to receive because that day was a day for grace.

Each child was allowed to choose something they had been wanting (within limits of course) and we would purchase it with them so that they could enjoy it, no strings attached. As parents, we also allowed ourselves to enjoy giving gifts without having to ask ourselves if we were spoiling our kids or not preparing them for real life.

I have found over the years that I am naturally inclined to distribute justice. Recently I've recognized that this probably has something to do with the way I was raised. I had a wonderful childhood and my parents are incredible people. I am very blessed to have been born into my family and to have been surrounded by people who loved and cared about me. They were examples of holy living in the midst of an inner-city ethnic neighborhood during the '70s race riots. As one of the few Caucasian families on the block, they continued to reach out to our neighbors in loving ways.

Maybe it was my personality that caused me to pay attention to the rules and the requirements of being a Christian that my parents taught me, as opposed to seeing how much grace they offered. I was a "good holiness girl" being raised by "good holiness parents" and I knew that God was a holy God who called us to be holy. "Without holiness no one shall see the Lord" (Hebrews 12:14) was branded onto my mind. I was determined to pursue it with every inch of my being.

This created a scary version of God for me. I knew that He loved me, but He had some pretty high expectations. This caused a great deal of fear during what I call the "I wish we'd all been ready" years. My mom was nearly always home after school, but on the rare day when she would not be there when I arrived, I would be convinced that the rapture had come and that I had been left behind because of some sin that I had forgotten to confess. Larry Norman's words would come bursting into my mind, "*Children died, the days grew cold, a piece of bread could buy a bag of gold... I wish we'd all been ready.*" I would frantically search the house and yard, my heart pounding, until finally I found her and could breathe again.

Fortunately my faith has matured a bit since I was 13 and I have now found a balance. I understand that with God, every day is "Grace and Mercy Day" and my efforts to please God are simply an out-flowing of my relationship with Him and my gratitude for the grace that He has given me.

Being the parent of children with special needs has opened my eyes much further in what it must feel like to be God. Our behavior as messed up, broken people is much like that of teenagers. We can treat Him, with our actions, as if He is invisible or non-existent. We don't do as He asks. We don't express gratitude for all He does for us. We are disrespectful, negligent, lazy and rude. We blame Him for everything, and sometimes even take our anger out on Him.

Today's good news is that there is no last straw with God. He doesn't fall into a heap in tears because we have pushed Him too far. He doesn't conclude that it's time for revenge, justice and punishment when we screw up. He sees our hearts and always approaches us from the side of grace.

Now I can already hear you theologians out there protesting and wanting to jump all over this and talk about the Old Testament and current religious thought and Wesley and Calvin and, and, and... but shhh. Let's not go there. Let's focus on what we agree on. God extended His mercy and grace to us while we were YET SINNERS. (Romans 5:8). And it is freely offered to us every day.

Have you had one of those weeks where you keep messing up and you are beginning to wonder if God is going to start giving you what you deserve? Are you thinking finally this might be that time where God screams ENOUGH?

Well guess what? It's never going to happen. Every time you come to Him, He is going to be there waiting to offer you mercy and grace. He has no last straw. While God never errs, He always approaches us from the side of grace. Jesus took upon himself our sin and our punishment so that we may be offered God's love instead. Take some time to ponder the fact that God's grace is limitless and that he will never say "ENOUGH"!

15

Grace Leads to Grace

Very aware of the fact that the title of this chapter may not seem to fit at all with the story I am about to tell, I am praying that you will bear with me to see that it all fits together in the end.

The night before the writing of this chapter, my husband had to call the jail and leave a message for our 21-year-old son. Six days before Christmas he left a message that our son would not be allowed to move back into our home. Having spent eight months of our last year allowing him, between jail stays, to be in our home, we have had to make a very difficult decision. We have never adopted children to have them end up homeless, so we have taken most of the 20 days of his sentence to look long and hard at what we would do next.

Over the past eight months he has not complied with the rules of our home. Nothing would convince him to live by the most simple guidelines (no girls in your bed overnight, for example) and his presence caused a great deal of stress for all who live here. We are people of grace. At least we attempt to be, so we trudged onward. We have finally realized that the cost to our other 9 children living here would be too great to allow him to return home.

Being a recipient of God's grace leads us to extend grace to others. While it may not seem that we are extending that grace to him, there is another part of this story that I hope will help you understand my need to share this sad fact with you.

Before we adopted children I found myself being a very judgmental person. If I saw a four-year-old having a temper tantrum in Wal-Mart, it was because the parents weren't strict enough at home. If a nine-year-old was a whiner, it was because the parents gave in too much. If I was driving down inner-city streets I would look at a young adult sleeping in an alley and think, "Wow, what kind of parents could allow this to happen to their child?" I would look at pregnant teenagers and wonder why their parents hadn't explained abstinence to them. My list of judgmental conclusions goes on and on and on.

Because my husband is a minister, it has always seemed important to us to have children who can be well behaved in public. However, this has not been the case. In fact, we have had a son who announced in a way too loud voice while his dad was preaching that he couldn't sit still because his Dad was too "F****" boring!" Because our kids have special needs that lead to multiple behavioral challenges, we have had to learn to swallow our pride, apologize for their misdeeds, and trust people to give us the benefit of the doubt.

Our congregation was severely tested, however, during one particular week about two years ago. During that one week three things happened. Our son, then 17, was caught after having stolen the cash out of the offering plate for several weeks. Our daughter, then 16, decided that even though we could make her go to church, we couldn't make her enter the sanctuary, and so she sat on a chair right outside the door glaring at everyone as they entered. Finally, the above-mentioned adult son who can no longer live at home broke into the church, stole the church safe (which he was never able to open) and did thousands of dollars of damage to the carpet as he was dragging the safe through the building. He wasn't living with us at the time, but it was definitely a personal blow to us and he knew it.

Much to our relief, our congregation demonstrated grace to us. They were forgiving and encouraging and showed understanding in the midst of things that monetarily cost them. They were willing to see things from a different perspective and offer grace to us. We could feel God's grace being expressed through them.

Since then, I have noticed my perspective changing. When I see children, teens and young adults who struggle, I extend grace to their parents. It may not even be an outward thing, but I internally am more willing to give them the benefit of the doubt. I accept the grace given to me by other people and extend it to others.

Recently I was the recipient of God's grace in a very real, personal, specific and significant way and I found the same thing happening. When I fully understood that God loved me and was extending his grace to me no matter what, I found myself extending more grace to the people around me. It became a natural out-flowing of the grace I had received.

If you have been a recipient of God's grace, I know the same will happen to you. A full understanding of God's grace can only lead us to offer it to others, freely, the way God offers it to us. No one who has authentically experienced God's grace can withhold it from others. Grace leads to grace.

Recently a very gifted communicator led Children's Time for the kids at our church. She put towels on the floor to protect the carpet and then put a basin of water on the floor. She invited the kids to play in it.

Our son Wilson and his buddy, another fifth grader, refused to touch the water. They observed things from afar, being way too cool to get involved. The third and fourth graders were tentative. They reached fingertips into the water and touched it to satisfy the enthusiastic woman who was begging them to enjoy the water. The first and second graders were a little less inhibited and allowed the water to flow through their hands and the preschoolers even played in it a bit.

There was a two-year-old in front whose mom had accompanied him. He couldn't get enough of that water. His mom couldn't hold him back. He splashed in it, rubbed it on his face, poured handfuls of it on his head. He then began to splash his four-year-old brother and those around him. He giggled. He laughed. The smile on his face was contagious as he joyfully played in the water.

During this scene which was so amazing to watch, we heard it explained that the water represented God's grace. He offers it to us and it is our choice what we are going to do with it. We can be a quiet observer of His grace or we can jump in and cover ourselves with it.

Having been the recipient of grace, God's grace as well as the grace of others, I am determined to spend my life not only playing in God's grace, but splashing it on others as well.

What about you? Would you like to join me? Can you come to the fountain and play in God's grace, rub it in your face and pour it on your head? Can you giggle, laugh and smile as you splash everyone you meet with the life-giving water of God's grace?

Let's do it. Let's fill our lives and the world around us with a steady flow of God's amazing grace.